**BIOLOGY Field Notes**

# Be a SCORPION Expert

by
Alex Hall

Minneapolis, Minnesota

**Credits**
All images are courtesy of Shutterstock.com, unless otherwise specified. With thanks to Getty Images, Thinkstock Photo, and iStockphoto.

Recurring – yana shypova, vectorplus, NotionPic, Diqdaya, The_Pixel, Milano M, Macrovector, Dmytro Vikarchuk, lineartestpilot, Oleksandra Klestova. Character throughout – NotionPic. Cover – Diqdaya, The_Pixel, Milano M, Macrovector, Dmytro Vikarchuk, lineartestpilot, Oleksandra Klestova, ingehogenbijl, Protasov AN. 4–5 – Vaclav Sebek, Chaikom. 6–7 – EcoPrint, SIMON SHIM. 8–9 – Chantelle Bosch, TaufikPho. 10–11 – Wirestock Creators, M Harits Fadhli. 12–13 – Vaclav Sebek, Artsiom P, Pike-28. 14–15 – Ernie Cooper, Janine Potgieter, Danita Delimont, Liz Weber. 16–17 – FJAH, Lauren Suryanata. 18–19 – Breck P. Kent, EcoPrint. 20–21 – Charly Morlock, RealityImages, Kurit afshen. 22–23 – Milan Zygmunt, Ernie Cooper, sbayram.

**Bearport Publishing Company Product Development Team**
Publisher: Jen Jenson; Director of Product Development: Spencer Brinker; Managing Editor: Allison Juda; Editor: Cole Nelson; Associate Editor: Naomi Reich; Associate Editor: Tiana Tran; Designer: Kim Jones; Designer: Kayla Eggert; Designer: Steve Scheluchin; Production Specialist: Owen Hamlin

Library of Congress Cataloging-in-Publication Data is available at www.loc.gov or upon request from the publisher.

ISBN: 979-8-89577-009-2 (hardcover)
ISBN: 979-8-89577-440-3 (paperback)
ISBN: 979-8-89577-126-6 (ebook)

© 2026 BookLife Publishing
This edition is published by arrangement with BookLife Publishing.

North American adaptations © 2026 Bearport Publishing Company. All rights reserved. No part of this publication may be reproduced in whole or in part, stored in any retrieval system, or transmitted in any form or by any means, electronic, mechanical, photocopying, recording, or otherwise, without written permission from the publisher. Bearport Publishing is a division of FlutterBee Education Group.

For more information, write to Bearport Publishing, 5357 Penn Avenue South, Minneapolis, MN 55419.

# CONTENTS

Meet the Biologist............4
A Scorpion's Body ...........6
Dinner Time...................10
Vicious Venom ...............12
Super Survivors..............14
Scorpion Stories .............16
Desert Homes ................18
Life Cycle......................20
Strong Scorpions............22
Glossary.......................24
Index ..........................24

# MEET THE BIOLOGIST

Hello! My name is Scarlet Scorpio, and I am a **biologist**. I have traveled the world to learn all I can about scorpions. They are amazing critters!

4

# A SCORPION'S BODY

Scorpions are invertebrates (in-VUR-tuh-brits). This means they do not have backbones. In fact, they do not have any bones in their bodies at all. Instead, scorpions have hard coverings called exoskeletons on their bodies.

An old exoskeleton

Scorpions **shed** their exoskeletons so their bodies can continue to grow.

The sharp tip of a scorpion's tail is called a stinger. This tip is filled with **venom**. Some scorpions can make their tails fall off to escape danger. However, this means that the critters lose their stingers.

A stinger

Scorpions poop from their tails. Once their tails are gone, they can no longer poop!

Pincers

Instead of hands, scorpions have pincers. These clawlike parts are used to catch and crush small **prey**. Scorpions also use their pincers to hold onto larger creatures. This allows scorpions to deliver their nasty sting.

Scorpions have tiny hairs on their legs called setae (SET-ay) that help them walk across sand without sinking in.

Scorpions are arachnids (uh-RAK-nidz), like spiders. This means they have eight legs. With so many legs, scorpions can run as fast as 12 miles per hour (19 kph). This helps them catch their meals and avoid being dinner themselves.

# DINNER TIME

When it is time to eat, most scorpions hide in small spaces to wait for their prey. Once the meal is near, scorpions quickly grab it with their pincers. The critters then sting their prey and inject their deadly venom.

Scorpions feed mostly on bugs and small animals.

10

Most scorpions hunt at night. They can sense movement on the ground to find their prey. But scorpions must be careful to not become food themselves. They have many **predators**, including meerkats, bats, and some mice.

A meerkat eating a scorpion

A pallid bat

Some predators are not affected by a scorpion's venom.

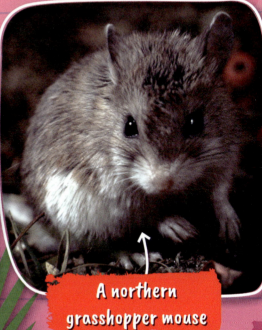

A northern grasshopper mouse

# VICIOUS VENOM

There are almost 2,000 different types of scorpions in the world. Luckily, not all of them are dangerous. Most scorpion stings are not deadly. Scientists say only 25 types of scorpions have venom strong enough to kill humans.

Most scorpions do not sting unless they are attacked.

The deathstalker is one of the most dangerous scorpions to humans. This animal lives in deserts in western Asia and northern Africa. A deathstalker may be small, but its venom can be deadly.

Don't worry! There is an **antivenom** for most scorpion stings.

# SUPER SURVIVORS

Scorpions have been around for a long time. Because scientists have found scorpion fossils, they know the creatures lived during the time of dinosaurs. That makes scorpions super survivors!

Fossils are the remains of plants and animals that have turned into rocks.

A scorpion fossil

14

Some scorpions have even survived after being frozen overnight and defrosted the next day.

When their food supply is low, scorpions have clever ways of staying alive. They can adjust their bodies to live on tiny amounts of food. Scorpions do this by slowing their breathing and living off as few as one bug in a year.

# SCORPION STORIES

In old Greek stories, scorpions often do very bad things. These tales show the critters harming other animals, including humans.

# DESERT HOMES

Most scorpions live in desert habitats. They can also be found in mountains, forests, and savannas. Scorpions live mostly alone in their hidden homes.

A habitat is the place where a plant or animal lives.

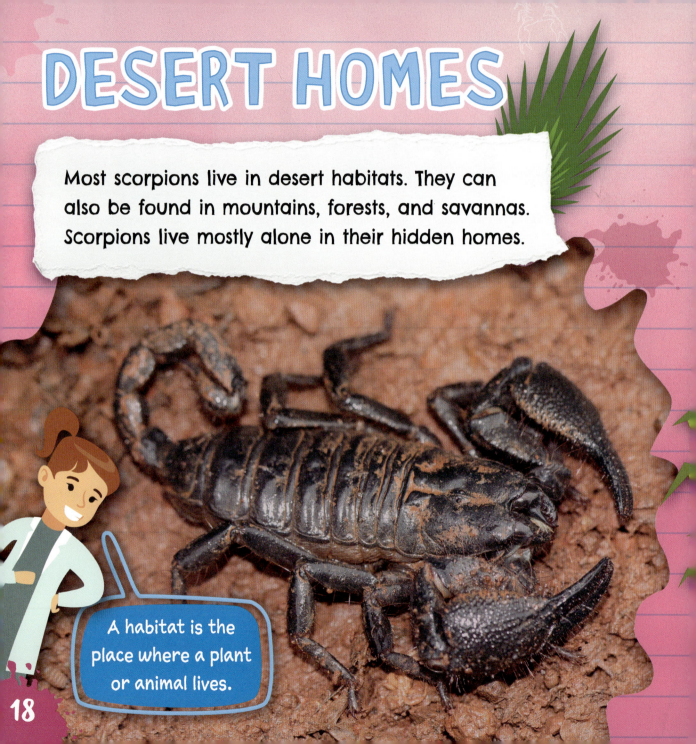

During the day, scorpions usually avoid the heat and light. Since they are nocturnal creatures, the critters are active mostly at night. To study scorpions in the dark, scientists use a special light that makes the creatures glow.

# LIFE CYCLE

The scorpion life cycle begins with a **male** and **female** coming together in the spring. A male scorpion may travel very far to find a partner. The female lets out a smell that helps the male find her.

A male scorpion

A life cycle includes the different stages of an animal's life.

Once they find each other, the scorpions lock their pincers and dance together. While dancing, they find somewhere flat on the ground to **mate**. Later, the female scorpion gives birth to as many as 100 babies!

Baby scorpions

Scorpions live for about 3 to 8 years in the wild.

# STRONG SCORPIONS

From piercing pincers to super stingers, scorpions are strong creatures! I hope you've enjoyed learning about these amazing critters.

# GLOSSARY

**antivenom** a medicine that blocks the effects of venom

**biologist** a person who studies and knows a lot about living things

**expert** a person who knows a lot about something

**female** a scorpion that can give birth

**male** a scorpion that cannot give birth

**mate** to come together to have young

**predators** animals that hunt other animals for food

**prey** animals that are hunted and eaten by other animals

**shed** to release an old skin when a new one grows

**venom** a poison from an animal that is usually passed on by a bite or sting

# INDEX

**deserts** 13, 18
**dinosaurs** 14
**exoskeletons** 6
**fossils** 14

**humans** 12–13, 16
**legs** 9
**pincers** 8, 10, 21–22
**predators** 11

**prey** 8, 10–11
**stingers** 7, 22
**tails** 7
**venom** 7, 10–13